Helsinki Travel Guide 2025

Where Silence Speaks Louder Than Monuments: A Contrarian's Guide to the Nordic Anti-Paradise

Madeline Houston

Table of Content

Chapter 9

THE HELSINKI EFFECT

INTRODUCTION TO HELSINKI

Brief History

I still remember my first glimpse of Helsinki's harbor, the morning sun glinting off the Baltic as my ferry approached from Stockholm. Little did I know then how deeply this city's unique history would captivate me.

Helsinki wasn't always Finland's capital. Founded in 1550 by Swedish King Gustav Vasa, it began as a modest trading town, intended to compete with the Hanseatic city of Tallinn across the Gulf. For centuries, it remained relatively insignificant, overshadowed by the older city of Turku. The turning point came in 1809, when Finland passed from Swedish to Russian control. Tsar Alexander I elevated

Helsinki to capital status in 1812, envisioning a grand imperial city worthy of his expanding empire.

Under Russian rule, Helsinki transformed. Architect Carl Ludwig Engel designed a new city center that would remind many of St. Petersburg, with its neoclassical buildings centered around Senate Square. The magnificent white Helsinki Cathedral, completed in 1852, still dominates the city skyline today – I've spent countless evenings sitting on its steps, watching the sunset paint the surrounding buildings in golden hues.

Finland's path to independence was tumultuous. The Russian Revolution of 1917 provided the opportunity for Finland to declare independence on December 6th of that year, but was quickly followed by a brief yet brutal civil war. Walking through the peaceful streets today, it's hard to imagine the conflicts that once divided this nation.

The 20th century brought more challenges – the Winter War and Continuation War against the Soviet Union forced Finland to cede territory but maintain sovereignty. Helsinki hosted the 1952 Summer Olympics, announcing Finland's arrival on the world stage. I once met an elderly gentleman at Café Regatta who remembered those games vividly, describing how the entire city seemed to vibrate with newfound optimism.

Since joining the European Union in 1995, Helsinki has established itself as a forward-thinking capital, embracing technology, design, and sustainability. The Nokia phenomenon of the 1990s and early 2000s put Finland on the global technology map, and though that particular chapter has closed, Helsinki's startup scene continues to thrive.

Geography and Climate

Helsinki occupies a peninsula and surrounding islands jutting into the Gulf of Finland. The city's intimate relationship with water became clear to me during my first summer here, when it seemed everyone was either sailing, swimming, or simply sitting by the shore. With over 300 islands within the city limits, Helsinki's archipelago setting creates a unique maritime character I've found in few other capital cities.

The city sprawls across gentle hills, none too steep, making it pleasantly walkable. Its highest natural point, Malminkartanonhuippu, rises just 90 meters above sea level – I climbed it one winter morning to find locals sledding down its snow-covered slopes, steam rising from their thermoses of hot chocolate.

Helsinki's climate taught me the true meaning of seasonal contrast. Winters are long and dark, with temperatures often dropping below -15°C (5°F) in January and February. The sun barely peeks above the horizon during December's shortest days, offering only 6 hours of weak daylight. I'll never forget my first winter solstice, when the city seemed to compensate for nature's darkness with thousands of twinkling lights.

Summer transforms Helsinki completely. During the height of summer, daylight stretches for nearly 19 hours. Temperatures typically range from 15-25°C (59-77°F), occasionally reaching 30°C (86°F) during heatwaves. These endless summer days have led to some of my most memorable experiences – midnight picnics in Kaivopuisto Park, watching the pink sky reflect in the harbor at 11 PM.

Spring arrives late but explosively, with the city's mood lifting noticeably as daylight hours increase and snow melts. Autumn paints the city in russets and golds, though the beautiful fall colors quickly give way to November's characteristic grayness and drizzle – a time when Finns retreat to their beloved cafés and saunas.

Best Time to Visit

The question I'm most frequently asked is when to visit Helsinki, and my answer has evolved over years of experiencing this city through all its seasons.

Summer (June-August) offers Helsinki at its most vibrant and accessible. Locals emerge from winter hibernation to fill outdoor terraces, markets, and beaches. The city hosts numerous festivals, including Flow Festival and Helsinki

Festival, bringing music and arts to various venues. Midsummer (Juhannus) in late June sees many residents leave for countryside cottages, making this a quieter period in the city – though those who remain celebrate with bonfires and festivities at places like Seurasaari Island.

I've found June and August ideal for balancing pleasant weather with smaller crowds. July brings the peak tourist season and occasional humidity, though temperatures rarely become uncomfortable. Summer allows exploration of the outer archipelago through public ferries, a truly magical experience as you hop between islands filled with traditional Finnish summer cottages.

Winter (December-February) transforms Helsinki into a different city entirely. Christmas markets, particularly the St. Thomas Market in

Senate Square, create a fairytale atmosphere with their glowing lights and mulled wine (glögi) stands. February's Lux Helsinki bathes the city's buildings in spectacular light installations that slice through the winter darkness. For travelers prepared for cold, winter offers unique experiences like ice skating on frozen bays or witnessing the Baltic Sea freeze into an otherworldly landscape.

My personal favorite seasons are the transitions. Spring (April-May) brings an infectious energy as melting snow reveals the first crocuses and Finns celebrate May Day (Vappu) with picnics and sparkling wine in Kaivopuisto Park. Autumn (September-October) offers golden light reflecting off the sea, mushroom foraging in nearby forests, and cultural events as theaters and concert venues launch their new seasons.

If you're seeking the quintessential Helsinki experience, I recommend late August into early September, when summer warmth lingers but the tourist crowds thin. The sea remains warm enough for swimming at beaches like Hietaniemi, while restaurants are showcasing fresh local harvests. Plus, you'll find locals in a mellow mood, savoring the last precious moments before winter's return.

Chapter 1

Getting There and Around

Stepping into Helsinki felt like entering a modern yet warmly inviting embrace of Nordic culture. In this chapter, I'll share my journey through the myriad ways of arriving and navigating this vibrant city, recounting my personal experiences from the moment I set foot in Helsinki until I finally strolled along its charming streets.

Arriving by Air, Sea, and Rail

My first glimpse of Helsinki was from the window of my plane as I approached the bustling Helsinki-Vantaa Airport—a gateway that immediately impressed with its sleek design and efficiency. Arriving by air is the most common entry point for international travelers.

The airport itself is well-organized, with clear signage in multiple languages, ensuring that even after a long flight, you feel both welcomed and guided. The rapid transit links between the airport and the city center made my transition seamless. Whether you opt for the train or a direct bus, the connection is quick and hassle-free, setting the tone for the rest of your adventure.

For those who prefer a more scenic arrival, Helsinki's sea and rail options offer their own special charms. I remember taking a short ferry ride from Tallinn, where the gentle rocking of the boat and the cool sea breeze provided a prelude to Helsinki's unique blend of maritime heritage and modernity. The ferry terminal is a hub of activity, filled with both locals and travelers sharing stories of past journeys. Meanwhile, arriving by rail unveils yet another layer of Helsinki's accessibility. With direct trains from various parts of Finland and neighboring countries, rail travel in this region is punctual, comfortable, and offers picturesque views of the Finnish countryside—a reminder that sometimes the journey is just as rewarding as the destination itself.

Public Transportation System

Once in the city, I quickly discovered that Helsinki's public transportation system is a marvel of efficiency and user-friendliness. The entire city is interconnected by a network of trams, buses, and a metro that makes exploring every nook and cranny both simple and enjoyable. My favorite part was hopping on a tram that glided past a mix of historic buildings and modern architectural marvels, each stop revealing another facet of the city's character.

Navigating the system is remarkably straightforward. The smart ticketing system, available via mobile apps or traditional ticket machines, allows you to pay for your journey without any fuss. I often found myself engrossed in people-watching while waiting for the next tram, where the blend of commuters, students, and tourists painted a picture of Helsinki's diverse community. For newcomers, the clear signage and timely announcements in both Finnish and English add an extra layer of ease, transforming public transport into an enjoyable part of your daily adventure.

In the evenings, when the city transforms into a canvas of lights and reflections along the waterfront, the metro and buses extend their service to ensure that every part of the city remains accessible. The punctuality and frequency of these services give you the freedom to explore Helsinki at your own pace, whether you're in search of late-night cultural events or a quiet corner of the city to reflect on the day's discoveries.

City Bikes and Walking Routes

For a more intimate experience of Helsinki, nothing compares to exploring by foot or on a city bike. One of my most cherished memories was renting a bike on a sunny morning and cycling through the tree-lined avenues and along the serene waterfront. Helsinki is a remarkably bike-friendly city, with dedicated lanes that wind through lush parks and alongside bustling urban centers. The ease of renting a bike—often through intuitive mobile apps—means that you can set off on your own adventure without the constraints of a car or bus schedule.

If biking isn't your preferred mode of
Helsinki's well-planned walking routes offer an
equally enchanting alternative. I found that
walking through neighborhoods like Punavuori
or the artistic district of Kallio provided a deeper
connection with the local culture. Every cobbled
street and hidden alleyway told a story, from the
quaint cafés serving freshly brewed coffee to the
vibrant street art that speaks of Helsinki's
youthful spirit. Walking here is not just about
covering distances; it's about immersing
yourself in the city's rhythm. I often took
leisurely strolls along the Esplanadi park, where
the mingling scents of fresh pastries and sea air
created an atmosphere of relaxed urban charm.

Whether you're pedaling along the scenic routes
or wandering through the historical layers of the
city on foot, Helsinki offers a perfect blend of
modern infrastructure and intimate local vibes.

Every journey, every step, unfolds a new story, making it not just a travel guide but a collection of personal adventures that weave together the rich tapestry of Helsinki life.

In sharing these experiences, I hope to convey how every mode of transportation in Helsinki isn't merely a means to get from point A to B, but rather a pathway to discovering the soul of the city. So pack your bags, lace up your walking shoes, and get ready to embark on a journey that's as much about the ride as it is about the destination.

Chapter 2

Where to Stay in Helsinki

Helsinki, the vibrant capital of Finland, offers a diverse range of accommodations to suit every traveler's needs, from luxurious retreats to budget-friendly hostels. Whether you're seeking opulence, a mid-range haven, or an affordable place to rest, Helsinki has something for everyone.

Luxury Accommodations

For those who desire the finest in comfort and elegance, Helsinki's luxury hotels are unparalleled. Here are some of the top choices:

- Hotel Kämp: Located in the heart of Helsinki, by the Esplanadi Park, Hotel Kämp is renowned for its luxurious amenities and stunning location. It has been a favorite among world leaders and celebrities, offering the most expensive suite in Finland, the Mannerheim Suite. Guests enjoy free parking and a complimentary airport shuttle.

- Lapland Hotels Bulevardi: Situated in the stylish Punavuori district, this hotel brings a touch of Lapland to Helsinki. Rooms are adorned with reindeer horns and Lappish textiles, and many feature private saunas. The hotel's breakfast buffet includes Lappish delicacies, adding to its unique charm.

- Hotel Lilla Roberts: This elegant art deco hotel in Kaartinkaupunki is praised for its spacious rooms and excellent service. It offers a luxurious stay with easy access to central attractions.

- Hotel St George: Known for its stylish rooms and calming ambiance, Hotel St George features a bakery and spa. Its Wintergarden Bar is a perfect spot to unwind, and it's just a short walk from the Kauppatori Market Place.

Mid-range Hotels

For travelers seeking quality without the luxury price tag, Helsinki's mid-range hotels offer excellent value:

- Scandic Grand Central Helsinki: Located inside the historic Helsinki Railway Station, this hotel offers a prime location with easy access to major attractions and transportation links. It welcomes pets in some rooms and includes a wonderful breakfast buffet.

- Hotel Helka: Situated between Kamppi and Töölö, Hotel Helka is a trendy, eco-friendly hotel with a Finnish sauna and complimentary breakfast featuring local delicacies.

- Sokos Hotel Presidentti: Near the Kamppi shopping center, this hotel offers themed rooms inspired by Finnish nature. It features a sauna and pool area, making it ideal for families and those seeking a local cultural experience.

- Hobo Hotel Helsinki: Located on Kluuvikatu, Hobo Hotel combines modern design with community-oriented spaces. It offers stylish rooms, a vibrant bar, and event spaces, making it perfect for travelers looking for a lively atmosphere.

Budget Options and Hostels

For travelers on a tighter budget, Helsinki provides a variety of affordable accommodations:

- Hostels: Helsinki has several hostels that offer dorms and private rooms at budget-friendly prices. These are great for backpackers and those looking to meet fellow travelers.

- Budget Hotels: Options like Hotel Finn in Kamppi offer simple yet cool accommodations close to the city center. Another choice is Hotel Arthur, which provides a charming stay with a great breakfast in the heart of Kluuvi.

Neighborhood Guide

Helsinki's neighborhoods each have their unique charm and advantages for travelers:

- Kluuvi: The heart of Helsinki's city center, Kluuvi is home to luxury hotels like Hotel Kämp and modern design hotels such as GLO Hotel Kluuvi. It's close to shopping streets and the Esplanadi Park.

- Kamppi: Known for its vibrant atmosphere, Kamppi hosts trendy hotels like Hotel Helka and Hotel Finn. It's a hub for shopping and dining, with easy access to public transport.

- Punavuori: This stylish district is home to Lapland Hotels Bulevardi and offers a mix of boutique shops and restaurants.

It's a bit quieter than Kamppi but still centrally located.

- Kaartinkaupunki: This upscale area features elegant hotels like Hotel Lilla Roberts and Hotel Fabian. It's known for its beautiful architecture and proximity to central attractions.

- Kallio: A bit further from the city center, Kallio offers a more laid-back atmosphere with stylish boutique hotels like Scandic Paasi. It's close to the metro and waterfront views.

Each neighborhood in Helsinki offers a distinct experience, ensuring that visitors can find the perfect place to stay based on their preferences and budget. Whether you're looking for luxury, mid-range comfort, or budget-friendly options,

Helsinki has something to suit every traveler's needs.

Chapter 3

Essential Experiences

Every moment in Helsinki felt like an invitation to discover something truly remarkable, and in my time exploring the city, a few experiences stood out as absolute essentials—each an emblem of the city's soul.

Helsinki Cathedral and Senate Square

I still remember my first sight of the Helsinki Cathedral, its gleaming white façade rising majestically over Senate Square. As I approached, I was captivated by the grandeur and the sense of history that emanated from its classic architecture. The cathedral, with its towering green domes and intricate details, seemed almost otherworldly against the backdrop of a clear blue sky. Walking through Senate Square, I couldn't help but feel transported to an era of imperial splendor. The square itself was alive with stories—cobbled stones that had witnessed centuries of change, flanked by neoclassical buildings that whispered secrets of Finland's past. Sitting on a bench in the square, I spent a quiet moment just soaking in the profound atmosphere, imagining the myriad events that had shaped this iconic space over time.

Suomenlinna Sea Fortress

No visit to Helsinki could be complete without a journey to Suomenlinna, the majestic sea fortress that guards the entrance to the city. I caught a ferry on a bright morning, the crisp Baltic air mingling with my excitement as the boat set off toward the fortress. The ride itself was a delightful prelude, offering panoramic views of Helsinki's coastal charm. Upon arrival, I found myself wandering through the maze of old fortifications and military tunnels, each corner steeped in history and brimming with tales of battles and alliances. The island's peaceful ambiance and its blend of natural beauty with architectural ingenuity left me in awe. I spent hours exploring its hidden nooks— discovering quaint museums, cozy cafés, and stunning vistas that looked out over the archipelago. It was a journey not just through space, but through time, revealing layers of Finnish resilience and creativity.

Design District

Helsinki's creative pulse beats strongest in its Design District—a vibrant, ever-changing canvas of artistic expression and modern innovation. As I meandered through the streets of this eclectic neighborhood, I was struck by the harmonious fusion of old and new. Galleries, boutiques, and design studios showcased the best of Finnish craftsmanship, where traditional techniques met contemporary visions. Every shop window, every art installation, told a unique story. I spent delightful afternoons chatting with local designers, each conversation offering a glimpse into the creative process and the passion behind every piece. The district wasn't just a place to shop; it was an immersive experience, inviting you to see the world through the eyes of those who shape it. I found myself inspired by the blend of minimalist elegance and bold experimentation—a true testament to Helsinki's reputation as a design capital.

Sauna Culture

Perhaps one of the most soul-soothing experiences was immersing myself in Finland's beloved sauna culture. It's one thing to read about the ritual, but it's entirely another to feel the heat, embrace the steam, and let go of all the world's worries. I visited a traditional public sauna, where locals and visitors alike gathered to experience a ritual that has been a cornerstone of Finnish life for generations. The warm, enveloping heat was both invigorating and calming, inviting deep, reflective moments. I savored the quiet intimacy of the experience— the way the sauna room pulsed with a gentle heat that seemed to wash away stress and invite a sense of unity with nature. In that simple yet profound setting, conversations flowed naturally, and for a while, the fast pace of modern life melted away. It was an experience that reconnected me with a timeless tradition, offering a glimpse into the Finnish way of finding balance and renewal.

Each of these experiences—whether standing before the grandeur of Helsinki Cathedral, exploring the storied walls of Suomenlinna, getting inspired in the Design District, or unwinding in a traditional sauna—told me a different facet of Helsinki's vibrant character. They weren't just attractions on a map; they were the heartbeat of the city, each beat echoing with history, creativity, and a deep respect for nature and community. Through these journeys, I discovered a Helsinki that was as multifaceted as it was welcoming, a city that effortlessly bridges its rich past with a bright, innovative future.

Chapter 4

FOOD AND DRINK

Traditional Finnish Cuisine

Finnish cuisine tells a story of a people deeply connected to their forests, lakes and harsh climate. My first encounter with traditional Finnish food came at Savotta restaurant near Senate Square, where I discovered how Finns have mastered the art of transforming simple ingredients into hearty, satisfying meals.

Finnish food revolves around pure flavors and local ingredients. Berries – cloudberries, lingonberries, blueberries – appear in both sweet and savory dishes. I've spent summer mornings foraging in Helsinki's surrounding forests, filling my basket with these jewel-like treasures, understanding why Finns hold their "everyman's right" to gather nature's bounty so dear.

Meat dishes reflect Finland's hunting traditions. Reindeer (poronkäristys) – served as thin slices sautéed with lingonberries and mashed potatoes – became an instant favorite of mine. Game meats like elk appear seasonally on menus, often accompanied by forest mushrooms and juniper berries.

Fish dominates coastal Helsinki's cuisine. Traditional gravlax (cured salmon), Baltic herring served a dozen ways, and creamy salmon soup (lohikeitto) showcase Finland's relationship with its waters. At Kauppatori market, I watched fishermen sell their morning catch directly from boats, and regularly treated myself to fried vendace (muikku) – small, crispy fish eaten whole with aioli.

Rye bread (ruisleipä) deserves special mention as Finland's culinary cornerstone. Dense, dark, and slightly sour, it's eaten at virtually every meal. The Karelian pasty (karjalanpiirakka) – a rye crust filled with rice porridge and topped with egg butter – makes for the perfect breakfast or snack. I found myself addicted to these at Hakaniemi Market Hall.

Don't miss these traditional dishes:

- Karjalanpaisti (Karelian stew) – a slow-cooked meat stew that warms the soul during winter

- Kaalikääryleet – cabbage rolls stuffed with rice and minced meat

- Kalakukko – fish baked inside a rye bread crust

- Leipäjuusto – "squeaky cheese" often served with cloudberry jam

- Korvapuusti – cinnamon buns spiced with cardamom

For brave palates, try memma (malted rye pudding) or salmiacki (ammonium chloride licorice) – both acquired tastes that Finns adore and foreigners often struggle with. My first encounter with salmiakki ice cream at Suomenlinna island left me gasping!

Market Halls and Food Markets

Helsinki's market halls and outdoor markets offer the most authentic food experiences in the city. These bustling hubs reveal the seasonal rhythms of Finnish cuisine and provide direct connections to producers.

Old Market Hall (Vanha Kauppahalli) Market Square houses historic wooden stalls under its vaulted ceiling. I spent countless lunch breaks here sampling Finnish cheeses, reindeer sausages, and fresh seafood. Soup+Victor serves exceptional fish soup, while Story offers modern Finnish small plates. The atmosphere – wood-paneled stalls, the mingling aromas of coffee and smoked fish – captures Helsinki's essence.

Hakaniemi Market Hall, recently renovated, spans two floors of food treasures in a less touristy setting. The ground floor features fresh produce, meats, and fish, while upstairs houses textiles, kitchenware, and casual cafés. Soppakeittiö's daily soups paired with fresh bread became my winter ritual.

For open-air markets, nothing beats Kauppatori (Market Square) on the harbor. From spring through fall, orange tents house vendors selling berries, vegetables, and prepared foods. The cauldrons of salmon soup steaming in the morning air create an irresistible invitation, even in drizzling rain. In winter, the Christmas Market transforms the square with glögi (mulled wine) and handcrafted gifts.

Hakaniemi Open-Air Market operates year-round, offering more reasonable prices than Kauppatori. Sunday mornings find locals browsing for mushrooms in autumn, fresh peas in summer, and chatting with farmers about their produce.

My personal ritual became visiting Teurastamo (the old abattoir district) for the monthly Street Food Carnival. This industrial-chic area hosts food trucks, pop-up restaurants, and urban gardens, showcasing Helsinki's evolving food scene.

Coffee Culture

Finland consumes more coffee per capita than any other nation in the world, and Helsinki's café scene reflects this deep cultural obsession. Coffee isn't just a beverage here – it's a way of life, a social institution, and for many Finns, a near-religious ritual.

The Finnish coffee tradition centers around kahvi and pulla – light, cardamom-spiced buns that perfectly complement the typically light-roasted, clear Nordic coffee. My first authentic coffee experience came at Café Regatta, a tiny red cottage on the waterfront where I squeezed onto a wooden bench, warming my hands around a bottomless cup while watching ice floes drift past in early spring.

Helsinki's traditional cafés, like Ekberg (Finland's oldest) and Fazer Café, maintain old-world elegance with their mirrored walls, marble tables, and magnificent pastry displays. At Fazer, I learned to order like a local – "kahvi ja korvapuusti" (coffee and cinnamon bun) – a combination that sustained generations of Helsinkians.

The third-wave coffee movement transformed Helsinki's scene in recent years. Good Life Coffee in Kallio, pioneered specialty beans and meticulous brewing methods. Baristas at Kaffa Roastery explained to me the distinct flavor profiles of their single-origin beans, while Sävy became my go-to for pour-overs prepared with scientific precision.

Johan & Nyström blends Scandinavian minimalism with coffee expertise, where I spent hours on their cushioned window seats watching snow fall while sampling their monthly specials. Andante serves exceptional micro-roasts alongside house-made pastries in their plant-filled space.

My favorite coffee discovery remains the summer café tradition. Seasonal spots like Mattolaituri and Café Ursula open only during warmer months, offering magnificent seaside settings to enjoy your brew. On mid-summer evenings, nursing an espresso while watching sailboats against the pink midnight sky became my definition of Helsinki magic.

Restaurant Recommendations

Helsinki's dining scene has exploded in recent years, earning international recognition while maintaining deep connections to Finnish ingredients and traditions. My explorations revealed everything from Michelin-starred establishments to hidden neighborhood gems.

For Nordic fine dining:

- Palace: Helsinki's Michelin-starred grand dame offering impeccable seasonal tasting menus with harbor views. Chef Eero Vottonen's langoustine with spruce oil and preserved berries revealed Finnish cuisine at its most sophisticated.

- Ora: Intimate 14-seat restaurant where I watched chefs prepare each course of a meticulously crafted tasting menu highlighting hyper-local ingredients.

- Grön: Toni Kostian's vegetable-forward restaurant changed my perception of plant-based Nordic cuisine with dishes like salt-baked celeriac with mushroom dashi.

For traditional Finnish:

- Juuri: Specializing in sapas (Finnish tapas), Juuri introduced me to modernized classics like vendace roe with sour cream on rye crisps.

- Savotta: Log cabin-style restaurant serving hearty classics in vintage Finnish dinnerware. Their archipelago fish platter with four preparations showcases coastal traditions.

- Konstan Möljä: All-you-can-eat Finnish buffet in a maritime-themed setting, where I first tried lanttulaatikko (rutabaga casserole) and other home-style dishes.

Market dining:

- Story: In Old Market Hall, offering modern Finnish small plates using ingredients from neighboring vendors.

- B-Smokery: Hakaniemi Market's hidden gem serving Finnish meat smoked on-site.

- E.Eriksson: Fish counter in Old Market Hall where I frequently grabbed gravlax sandwiches for waterfront picnics.

International standouts:

- Farang: Nordic-Southeast Asian fusion that became my special occasion destination for dishes like betel leaf wraps with smoked Arctic char.

- Basbas: Middle Eastern flavors meet Finnish ingredients in this lively spot near Kamppi center.

- Mamu: Georgian restaurant introducing Helsinki to khachapuri bread boats filled with egg and cheese.

- Via Tribunali: Naples-certified pizzeria that saved me on homesick evenings.

Budget-friendly favorites:

- Pompier Espa: Classic Finnish lunch spot serving daily specials for under €15.

- Fafa's: Local chain offering excellent falafel pitas.

- Lie Mi: Vietnamese street food stand in Hakaniemi Market serving remarkable pho.

- Soppakeittiö: Soup kitchen in Hakaniemi Market Hall offering daily soups with bread for €10.

For special dining experiences, check seasonal pop-ups like Meripaviljonki – floating on water during summer months – or book Nokka's chef's table, where I spent five unforgettable hours watching chefs transform local ingredients into edible art while explaining each technique and source.

Chapter 5

Seasonal Activities in Helsinki

Helsinki transforms beautifully with each passing season, offering unique experiences that cater to all tastes. Whether basking in the endless daylight of summer, embracing the frosty charm of winter, or enjoying the gentle transitions of spring and autumn, Helsinki's seasonal activities are a treasure trove waiting to be explored.

Summer in Helsinki

Summer in Helsinki is nothing short of magical. The city comes alive under the midnight sun, with long days and vibrant energy that seems to permeate every corner.

- Cultural Events and Festivals: Helsinki's cultural centres host a plethora of free events during summer. Annantalo offers art workshops for children and street art projects, while Kanneltalo organizes art camps that explore painting techniques inspired by nature. The summer culminates in the *Night of the Arts* in August, featuring performances by local bands, jazz orchestras, and even Venetian Carnival-themed block parties.

- Outdoor Concerts and Movies: Parks like Kaivopuisto transform into open-air cinemas during July and August, where classic films are screened under the stars. The Esplanade Park becomes a hub for Jazz-Espa, Finland's longest jazz festival, offering free live music throughout July.

- Nature Adventures: Helsinki's coastline and archipelago are perfect for water-based activities. Rent a paddleboard or kayak to explore Töölö Bay or sail through the archipelago on ferries that stop at picturesque islands. For sun-seekers, outdoor pools like Stadikka offer refreshing dips in the city's warm embrace.

- Alppipuisto Park Events: Weekends at Alppipuisto Park are filled with diverse music events such as Afrojazz Club performances and folk festivals. These gatherings foster a sense of community and showcase Helsinki's multicultural spirit.

Winter Wonderland

Winter in Helsinki is a time of serene beauty, where snow blankets the city and lights twinkle against the dark skies. Despite the cold, there is no shortage of activities to keep visitors enchanted.

- Sauna Culture: A quintessential Finnish experience is indulging in a sauna followed by an icy dip. Kulttuurisauna offers a tranquil setting near Merihaka, while Kuusijärvi provides smoke saunas with access to frozen lakes for an authentic experience.

- Christmas Markets: Starting in December, Christmas markets like Tuomaan Markkinat at Market Square feature handicrafts, mulled wine, and festive treats. These markets are perfect for soaking up holiday cheer while shopping for unique Finnish gifts.

- Outdoor Activities: Winter sports enthusiasts can enjoy cross-country skiing along groomed trails in Central Park or Paloheinä Forest. Ice skating rinks like Brahenkenttä offer rentals and cozy hot chocolate breaks afterward. Snowshoeing excursions through snowy forests provide opportunities for adventure and stunning photography.

- Frozen Archipelago Cruises: Hovercraft tours offer thrilling journeys across frozen seas, complete with survival suits for safety. Guests can enjoy barbecue lunches on ice while marveling at the stark beauty of Helsinki's winter landscape.

Spring and Autumn Experiences

Spring and autumn are transitional seasons that bring their own charm to Helsinki. These quieter months offer moments of reflection and discovery.

- Spring Awakening: As snow melts away, parks like Kaisaniemi come alive with blooming flowers. Spring is ideal for leisurely walks through Helsinki's Design District or along the waterfront promenades.

- Autumn Colors: Autumn paints Helsinki in hues of gold and crimson. It's a time for cozy café visits and exploring museums like Ateneum or Kiasma before heading outdoors to enjoy nature trails surrounded by falling leaves.

- Seasonal Food Markets: Both spring and autumn are marked by bustling food markets showcasing seasonal produce. Market Square becomes a hub for fresh berries in spring and hearty root vegetables in autumn.

Helsinki's seasonal activities ensure that no matter when you visit, there is always something captivating to experience. From summer's endless light to winter's frosty magic and the tranquil beauty of spring and autumn, this city offers unforgettable adventures year-round.

Chapter 6

Day Trips and Excursions

Helsinki is a brilliant gateway not only to its own treasures but also to a variety of unforgettable day trips and excursions. In my journeys outside the city, I discovered enchanting natural landscapes, charming historic towns, and even a touch of international allure—all just a short trip away.

Nuuksio National Park

One of my most rejuvenating escapes was a day spent in Nuuksio National Park. Leaving the urban buzz behind, I found myself immersed in a pristine wilderness where the rhythmic sounds of nature replaced the constant hum of city life. As I ventured into the park, towering pine trees and serene lakes framed my path, each turn revealing a scene more breathtaking than the last. I wandered along well-marked trails, occasionally pausing to marvel at the clear, still waters of hidden ponds. There was a sense of peace and timelessness that only nature can offer—a place where you can truly breathe. I even encountered some of Finland's native wildlife in its natural habitat, a reminder of the wild beauty that thrives just beyond Helsinki's edges. The crisp, fresh air filled my lungs, and I left the park with a deep sense of renewal and a heart full of memories.

Porvoo Old Town

A short drive east of Helsinki, Porvoo Old Town exudes a quaint charm that feels like stepping back in time. I arrived in Porvoo on a crisp morning, and immediately, the cobblestone streets, centuries-old wooden houses, and picturesque river views captivated my imagination. Wandering through the narrow lanes, I could feel the history beneath my feet, with every building and alleyway echoing stories from a bygone era. The town's vibrant atmosphere was further enhanced by cozy cafés and artisan boutiques, each offering local crafts and delicacies that invited me to linger a little longer. I spent hours exploring its hidden corners, absorbing the blend of rustic charm and artistic spirit that makes Porvoo so irresistible. It was a day of slow-paced discovery—a delightful reminder that sometimes, the simplest journeys are the most enriching.

Tallinn Ferry Trip

Perhaps the most adventurous of all was the ferry trip to Tallinn, which added an international flair to my travel narrative. Departing from Helsinki's bustling harbor, I boarded a modern ferry that promised both comfort and stunning views across the Baltic Sea. The journey was an experience in itself—a blend of the invigorating sea breeze, expansive ocean vistas, and a palpable sense of excitement as the shoreline of Estonia gradually came into view. On board, I mingled with fellow travelers, each sharing their own stories of discovery, which made the voyage feel like a moving community of explorers. Arriving in Tallinn was like entering a fairy tale, with its medieval architecture and cobblestone streets transporting me to another era. The ferry trip was more than just a means of travel—it was an integral part of my adventure, blending the thrill of international exploration with the ease and comfort of modern travel.

Every excursion from Helsinki offers its own unique chapter in your travel story. Whether you're trekking through the serene trails of Nuuksio, wandering the historic lanes of Porvoo, or embracing the sea-sprayed excitement of a Tallinn ferry trip, these day trips transform a simple getaway into a series of deeply personal, unforgettable experiences. Each journey not only enriches your understanding of the region but also leaves you with a lingering sense of wonder and a story to tell—a narrative of exploration that goes far beyond the city limits.

Chapter 7

Shopping Guide to Helsinki

Helsinki, renowned as a hub for design and innovation, offers a diverse shopping experience that caters to all tastes and preferences. From iconic Finnish design to unique souvenirs and bustling markets, the city is a shopper's paradise.

Finnish Design

Finnish design is celebrated globally for its simplicity, functionality, and beauty. Helsinki is home to numerous iconic design stores and districts that showcase the best of Finnish creativity.

- Design District Helsinki: Spanning across 25 streets in the city center, this district is a haven for design enthusiasts. It features a mix of galleries, boutiques, and design agencies, offering everything from jewelry to furniture. Visitors can explore local artisans and renowned establishments, making it a must-visit for anyone interested in Finnish design.

- Iconic Design Stores:

- Artek Helsinki: Known for Alvar Aalto's furniture designs, Artek is a must-visit for fans of modernist design. Located at Keskuskatu 1B, it offers a wide range of classic and contemporary pieces.

- Iittala & Arabia Store: Situated on Pohjoisesplanadi, this store showcases stunning glassware and ceramics from two of Finland's most beloved brands.

It's a perfect place to find beautiful souvenirs or gifts.

- Marimekko: With its flagship store on Norra Esplanaden, Marimekko is synonymous with vibrant Finnish textiles and fashion. The brand's bold prints and colorful designs make it a favorite among design enthusiasts.

- Design Museums and Events:

- Design Museum Helsinki: Located on Korkeavuorenkatu, this museum provides a comprehensive overview of Finnish design history and contemporary trends. It hosts seasonal exhibitions and events, making it a great resource for understanding the evolution of Finnish design.

- Helsinki Design Week: This annual festival celebrates design in all its forms, featuring exhibitions, talks, and markets across the city. It's an excellent opportunity to discover new design talents and trends.

Souvenirs and Handicrafts

For those looking to take a piece of Helsinki back home, the city offers a variety of unique souvenirs and handicrafts.

- Traditional Finnish Handicrafts: Visit local markets or specialty shops to find handmade items such as wooden crafts, woolen textiles, and ceramics. These make thoughtful gifts or personal mementos.

- Design Souvenirs: Stores like Iittala and Marimekko offer beautifully designed items that are quintessentially Finnish. From glass vases to colorful textiles, these souvenirs reflect the country's design heritage.

Markets and Shopping Centers

Helsinki's markets and shopping centers provide a lively atmosphere where visitors can find everything from fresh produce to high-end fashion.

- Markets:

- Market Square (Kauppatori): Located by the waterfront, this bustling market offers fresh seafood, local delicacies, and souvenirs. It's a great place to experience Helsinki's vibrant market culture.

- Old Market Hall (Vanha Kauppahalli): This historic hall features a variety of food stalls and specialty shops selling Finnish delicacies and handicrafts. It's a must-visit for foodies and those seeking authentic Finnish experiences.

- Shopping Centers:

- Kämp Galleria: Situated in the heart of Helsinki, Kämp Galleria offers a luxurious shopping experience with a mix of Finnish design brands and international fashion labels. It's a great place to find high-quality clothing and accessories.

- Forum Shopping Centre: Located near the city center, Forum features a wide range of stores, including Finnish design boutiques and international brands. It's a convenient spot for shopping and dining.

- Itis Shopping Centre: One of the largest shopping centers in the Nordic region, Itis offers a vast selection of stores and restaurants. It's a bit further from the city center but accessible by public transport.

Helsinki's shopping scene is a blend of tradition and innovation, making it an exciting destination for anyone interested in design, culture, and local experiences. Whether you're looking for iconic Finnish design, unique souvenirs, or vibrant market experiences, Helsinki has something to offer every kind of shopper.

Chapter 8

Sustainable Helsinki

Helsinki isn't just a modern metropolis—it's a city deeply committed to a sustainable future. In my explorations, I discovered that every corner of Helsinki breathes a passion for environmental stewardship, from innovative eco-friendly initiatives to expansive green spaces and a culture that champions responsible tourism. Let me take you through the story of how Helsinki is redefining urban life in harmony with nature.

Eco-friendly Initiatives

One of the first things that struck me upon arriving in Helsinki was the city's unwavering dedication to sustainability. Everywhere you look, there are subtle yet powerful reminders of innovative eco-friendly initiatives. As I roamed the streets, I noticed an impressive network of electric buses and trams silently weaving through the city, a tangible sign of Helsinki's investment in clean public transportation.

Local authorities have embraced cutting-edge technologies to reduce emissions and promote renewable energy, making sustainability not just an idea but a daily practice. For instance, the city's waste management system is a marvel in itself—sophisticated recycling programs, energy-from-waste plants, and community-driven composting initiatives that turn everyday waste into valuable resources. I found it fascinating to learn how local startups and municipal projects collaborate to bring forth green energy solutions, from solar panels on public buildings to pilot projects for geothermal energy. These initiatives are woven into the very fabric of city planning, making every journey through Helsinki a subtle reminder of how urban innovation can go hand in hand with environmental consciousness.

Green Spaces

Strolling through Helsinki, I quickly realized that green spaces are the soul of the city. Amid the modern architectural wonders, parks and gardens provide a serene escape from the urban rush. One of my favorite memories is spending a lazy afternoon in the expansive Central Park, where winding trails, towering trees, and quiet ponds created a perfect haven for reflection and recreation. The city's commitment to preserving natural areas is evident in the meticulous care taken to integrate lush parks within the urban landscape.

Every park in Helsinki seems to have its own unique personality—some echoing the historical charm of old European gardens, others offering a modern twist with minimalist designs and eco-friendly features. I was particularly impressed by how community gardens and urban farms are thriving, inviting locals and visitors alike to participate in sustainable living. These green spaces are not only vital for biodiversity but also serve as communal hubs where people gather, share stories, and celebrate the beauty of nature in an urban setting.

Responsible Tourism

Helsinki's approach to tourism goes beyond the typical visitor experience—it's about creating a dialogue between travelers and the local community while preserving the environment for future generations. Responsible tourism here is all about respect: respect for local culture, for the environment, and for the city's rich heritage.

Throughout my journey, I encountered tour operators who focus on low-impact travel, ensuring that every excursion contributes positively to the local economy and minimizes environmental footprints. Many tours incorporate lessons on Finnish traditions and the importance of sustainability, encouraging visitors to adopt greener practices during their stay. Whether it was cycling tours that allowed me to explore hidden neighborhoods at a leisurely pace or guided walks through historical sites with a focus on conservation, each experience was designed to immerse me in the city's eco-friendly ethos.

Local restaurants and cafés also proudly champion locally sourced ingredients and sustainable practices, a trend that not only enhances the culinary experience but also supports regional farmers and producers. In Helsinki, responsible tourism isn't a mere buzzword—it's a lived reality, an invitation to experience a city that takes pride in its efforts to protect both its cultural heritage and its natural beauty.

In every facet of Helsinki, from its visionary eco-friendly projects to its vibrant green spaces and heartfelt commitment to responsible tourism, I found a city that is as forward-thinking as it is grounded in tradition. As I journeyed through its sustainable landscapes, I realized that Helsinki isn't just a destination—it's an inspiring story of how urban living can thrive in balance with nature, a narrative that beckons travelers to be part of a movement toward a greener future.

Chapter 9

THE HELSINKI EFFECT

As I stand at the ferry terminal on my last evening in Helsinki, watching the golden Baltic sun cast long shadows across Kauppatori, I find myself unexpectedly emotional. How does a city work its way into your heart so completely, so quietly? The Finns have a word that captures this feeling perfectly: *kaiho* – a melancholic longing, a homesickness for a place that isn't technically home.

Helsinki never announces itself with grand gestures. It doesn't have Paris's iconic silhouette or Rome's ancient grandeur. Instead, it reveals itself in quiet moments: steam rising from a harborside sauna as snowflakes dance in winter twilight; the precise ritual of a barista preparing your morning coffee; the symphony of bicycle bells along Baana on the first proper spring day.

I came here initially as a visitor, guidebook in hand, checking landmarks off a list. Suomenlinna, Senate Square, Temppeliaukio Church – I dutifully photographed them all. But Helsinki slowly taught me to measure a city differently. The true pulse of this place beats in its rhythms and values: the work-life balance that sends office workers home by 4 PM; the trust that leaves baby carriages unattended outside cafés; the democratic spirit where CEOs and construction workers share sauna benches in companionable silence.

The seasons became my calendar, each with its distinct personality. Winter taught me the Finnish concept of *sisu* – that special resilience that propels people forward through darkness and cold. Summer brought the miracle of white nights when the city collectively celebrates light until 2 AM, making up for those December days when the sun merely suggests itself before disappearing again.

But perhaps Helsinki's greatest gift is its people. Beneath the stereotype of Finnish reserve lies extraordinary warmth. It simply operates on a different timeline than the instant friendliness of some cultures. My neighbor Matti spoke barely ten words to me during my first month in the Kallio apartment building. By year three, he was inviting me to his family's summer cottage, teaching me to fish through ice, and debating the finer points of Finnish literature over home-distilled spirits.

Helsinki works human connection into its urban fabric. Public saunas become social levelers, Oodi Library transforms learning into community experience, restaurant day turns apartments into pop-up eateries. There's a profound awareness that cities exist for people – all people – not merely as economic engines or tourist attractions.

I've changed here. The Finnish appreciation for simplicity has reshaped my sense of what's necessary and beautiful. Their relationship with nature – respectful but unsentimental – has altered how I spend weekends. Their trust in institutions reminds me that functional government isn't a fantasy but a choice societies make together.

As my ferry pulls away, Helsinki's skyline receding, I realize what makes this city extraordinary. In a world that increasingly values spectacle and consumption, Helsinki offers something radical: sufficiency. Enough beauty, enough innovation, enough connection – without excess. This city understands that true quality of life emerges not from constant stimulation but from balance, functionality, and measured pleasure.

The Finns have a saying: "Happiness doesn't come from searching for it, but from living." Perhaps that's Helsinki's lasting gift to travelers willing to slow down and absorb its lessons. You won't leave with a memory card full of landmark photos or stories of wild adventures, but with something more valuable: a recalibration of what matters.

I'll return, of course. To once again walk along the archipelago shoreline as evening light stretches across the water. To breathe the pine-scented air of Keskuspuisto forest after summer rain. To feel the particular warmth of stepping from winter streets into a café filled with candles and conversation.

Until then – *näkemiin*, Helsinki. Until we meet
again.

Dear Reader,

Thank you for choosing to explore my book. Your time and interest mean the world to me. I hoped this work not only offered practical tips and insights but also brought inspiration and joy to your travels. I aimed to capture the essence of every destination, inviting you to experience each awe-inspiring moment with me.

Your support inspires me to keep sharing my passion for travel and storytelling. If you enjoyed this book, I would be truly honored if you considered exploring more of my work in the future.

Thank you again for being such a valued reader. Wishing you countless adventures and unforgettable journeys ahead!

Printed in Dunstable, United Kingdom

66540411R00047